★ IT'S MY STATE! ★
Delaware

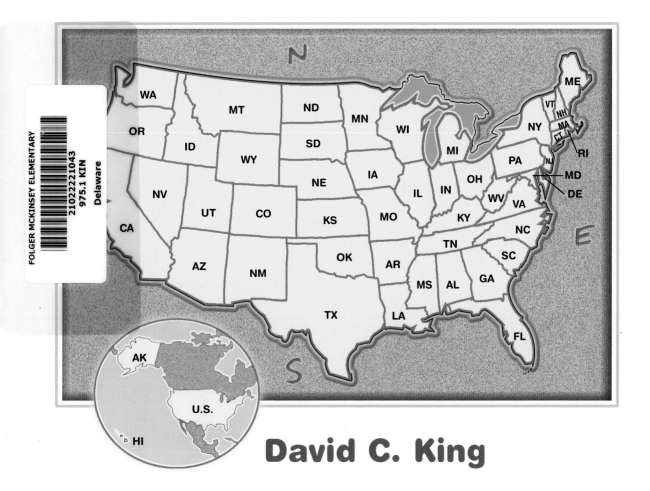

David C. King

BENCHMARK BOOKS

MARSHALL CAVENDISH
NEW YORK

Benchmark Books
Marshall Cavendish Corporation
99 White Plains Road
Tarrytown, New York 10591-9001
www.marshallcavendish.com

Maps, text, and illustrations copyright © 2005 by Marshall Cavendish Corporation
Maps and illustrations by Christopher Santoro

Library of Congress Cataloging-in-Publication Data

King, David C.
Delaware / by David C. King.
p. cm. — (It's my state!)
Includes bibliographical references and index.
ISBN 0-7614-1826-1
1. Delaware—Juvenile literature. I. Title. II. Series.

F164.3.K56 2004
975.1—dc22

Photo research by Candlepants, Inc.

Cover photo: Kevin Fleming / Corbis
Back cover illustration: The license plate shows Delaware's postal abbreviation, followed by its year of statehood.

The photographs in this book are used by permission and through the courtesy of: *Corbis:* 24, 32, 33, 67 (bottom); Martin B.
Withers / Frank Lane Picture Agency, 4 (bottom); Maurice Nimmo / Frank Lane Picture Agency, 5 (middle); Scott T. Smith, 5
(bottom); Kevin Fleming, 8, 11, 13, 14, 36, 38, 39, 43, 45, 49, 51, 60, 65, 66 (bottom), 67 (top), 69, 71, 72; Kit Kittle, 10; David
Muench, 12; Lynda Richardson, 17; Chase Jarvis, 18; Gary W. Carter, 23 (bottom); Stapleton Collection, 28, 46 (middle); Roger
Ressmeyer, 47 (middle); Jim Sugar, 48; Joseph Sohm/ChromoSohm Inc., 50; Lee Snider, 54; Paul A. Souders, 58; Roman Soumar,
67 (middle); Kristin Royalty, 70; Bettmann, 34, 35 (top), 35 (bottom), 46 (middle), 46 (bottom). *Photo Researchers, Inc.:* Jerry
Ferrara, 4 (top); John Bova, 22 (bottom); Blair Seitz, 66 (top). *Superstock:* ThinkStock, 5 (top); Phil Cantor, 9; Edward Cohen, 20.
Animals Animals / Earth Scenes: Robert Maier, 4 (middle); Michael Gadomski, 15; Zigmund Leszczynski, 16; Doug Wechsler, 22
(top); Daybreak Imagery, 23 (top). *Minden Pictures:* Tom Vezo, 22 (middle); Jim Brandenburg, 23 (middle). *North Wind Picture
Archives:* 26, 27, 30. *Getty Images:* 47 (bottom); Time Life Pictures, 47 (top). *The Image Works:* Joe Sohm, 52. *Index Stock:* Grant
Heilman Photography, 62; Jeff Greenberg, 66 (middle). *Envision:* RESO, 63.

Series design by Anahid Hamparian
Printed in Italy

1 3 5 6 4 2

Contents

A Quick Look at Delaware

Nickname: The First State

Population: 807,385 (2002 estimate)

Statehood: Dec. 7, 1787

Flower: **Peach Blossom**

About 1840, when Delaware farmers desperately needed a new crop, they found that peaches, imported from China, grew well in the sandy soil. The delicate peach blossom became a symbol of a new wave of prosperity. Since 1900, however, a blight called the "yellows" has drastically reduced the peach harvest.

Insect: Ladybug

In the 1970s, second-grade students from an elementary school in Milford led an effort to make this beetle the official state insect. In 1974 the ladybug was officially adopted as the state insect. Lady bugs can be found throughout the state.

Tree:
American Holly

The American holly tree has long been a symbol of the Christmas season, with its oblong, prickly leaves and bright red berries. They grow to a height of 60 feet or more.

Beverage: Milk

Milk was adopted as the official state beverage in 1983. Dairy farms have always been important to Delaware's economy. Milk from Delaware's cows is sold throughout Delaware and to other states and is used in products such as cheese, ice cream, and butter.

Fossil: Belemnite

In 1996, the belemnite was named Delaware's state fossil. Belemnites are sea creatures that are now extinct, which means that they no longer exist. But scientists know that belemnites are related to and looked a lot like certain types of modern-day squid. Belemnite fossils have been found in the coastal regions around the Chesapeake Bay.

Marine Animal: Horseshoe crab

Horseshoe crabs live in sandy or muddy regions near coastal waters. Delaware Bay has large populations of these marine animals. Each one has five pairs of legs and a spiky tail. These horseshoe-shaped crabs feed on worms, clams, and other small sea creatures. The horseshoe crab became Delaware's state marine animal in 2002.

1 The First State

If you travel along Ebright Road in Delaware's New Castle County, you might spot a highway sign marking the highest point in the state—an elevation of exactly 442 feet above sea level. That means that Delaware lies closer to sea level than any other state.

Delaware is a small state—only Rhode Island is smaller—and it has fewer people than forty-four other

Delaware's Borders
North: Pennsylvania
South: Maryland
East: Delaware River, Delaware Bay, and the Atlantic Ocean
West: Maryland

states. But, Delaware's history is packed with colorful events and reminders of America's past are everywhere in the state. Delaware is a state of great natural beauty, with countless opportunities for work and for recreation.

Three Counties, Two Regions

Delaware occupies part of the long Delmarva Peninsula—with Maryland and Virginia having the southern portions of the peninsula. In the late 1600s, three counties that were part of Pennsylvania asked to be separated from the rest of

7

William Penn's colony. Penn agreed and Delaware today consists of the same three counties—New Castle, Kent, and Sussex. Delaware has fewer counties than any other state. Roughly two-thirds of the people live in the northern county of New Castle, especially around Wilmington. The two southern counties are more rural and less heavily populated.

Delaware is home to acres of fertile farmland.

The city of Wilmington at night.

The name Delaware was first applied to the bay and the river by an English explorer, Samuel Argall, in 1610. He named the bodies of water in honor of Sir Thomas West, Lord De la Warr. West was serving as governor of Virginia—the only English colony in North America at the time. The name was later applied to the three counties on the western side of Delaware Bay and Delaware River.

When the northern border between Delaware and Pennsylvania was determined, a perfect circle was drawn on a map, with the the town of New Castle as the center. The border between Delaware and Pennsylvania is shaped like an arc because it is part of that circle. All sections of this border are supposed to be exactly 12 miles from New Castle.

The state has only two geographic regions. In the north, a narrow strip of land is part of a geographic region of North America called the Piedmont. This is an area of gently rolling hills found throughout the Atlantic Coast states east of the Appalachian Mountains. Most of Delaware is part of the Atlantic Coastal Plain—a narrow belt of lowland that extends from New York to Florida.

The coast itself in Delaware is a long sand beach stretching from the Maryland border in the north to Cape Henlopen at the mouth of Delaware Bay.

This lighthouse stands on Cape Henlopen on the Delaware Bay.

Although the ocean coastline is only 28 miles long, following all the inlets and bays makes it about a 300-mile coastline. Most of this beach is a low sand bar between the ocean and a series of lagoons and shallow

bays. At both Rehoboth Beach and Bethany Beach, the mainland reaches directly to the ocean. The sand beaches make this a popular tourist destination. In fact Rehoboth Beach is advertised as the closest resort area to Washington, D. C. In the southernmost part of the state, the land becomes marshy, forming the famous 30,000-acre Cypress Swamp, which is also known as the Great Pocomoke Swamp.

The state's border with Maryland runs through two towns with names that combine the names of the two states: Delmar and Marydel.

On warm sunny days, Bethany Beach is a popular spot for locals and visitors.

Cypress trees, moss, and other plants thrive in Delaware's swampy areas.

Delaware

A low sandy ridge extends north and south through the state just inside Delaware's western border. This ridge forms the state's watershed—the high ground where most of Delaware's rivers rise (or begin). The rivers and streams then flow east into Delaware Bay and the Atlantic Ocean, or west into Chesapeake Bay. Some of these rivers provided water power that ran mills throughout the 1800s, including the gunpowder mills that became Delaware's most important industry for a time. A human-made waterway—the Chesapeake and Delaware Canal—cuts across the state just south of Wilmington, connecting Delaware Bay and Chesapeake Bay. All of these waterways played a vital role in Delaware's economic development, establishing trade with major cities, especially Philadelphia and Baltimore.

Throughout Delaware's history, towns and cities have developed on the coasts of the state's bodies of water.

Climate

Delawareans throughout most of the state enjoy warm springs. But summer temperatures vary in different parts of the state. During the summer, coastal regions of Delaware tend be a little cooler than the rest of the state. This is because breezes from

In the fall, most trees in Delaware turn vivid shades of orange, red, and yellow.

the Atlantic Ocean bring cool air to the coast. Summers in most of the state can be humid with temperatures that average between 70 and 80 degrees Fahrenheit. But it can get hotter. The highest recorded temperature in Delaware's history occurred in Millsboro in July 1930. It was 110 degrees.

As summer passes and fall begins, the temperatures decrease. Leaves on trees begin to change colors and fall. Many visitors and residents enjoy hiking through parts of Delaware, enjoying the cooler weather and vivid colors of fall.

Winters in Delaware are not as harsh as winters in more northern states. The mountainous regions of Pennsylvania block cold northwestern winter winds from hitting Delaware. The average winter temperature is around 35 degrees. But it is not uncommon for the temperature to sometimes drop below freezing. On January 17, 1893, Millsboro recorded the state's lowest temperature. The thermometer dropped to a very chilly -17 degrees. Delaware does get snow in the wintertime, though it varies from the north to the south. Northern parts of the state receive about 17 inches of snow each year. Southern and coastal regions receive about 13 inches.

Plant and Animal Life

Because Delaware is in a middle zone between northern and southern plant life, there is a great variety of trees. Trees common to northern regions are abundant, including oak, maple, hickory, and poplar. Trees that are not found any farther north, such as bald cypress, sweet gum, and loblolly pine also thrive in Delaware.

From March to October, Delaware's level fields and meadows seem to be carpeted in wildflowers. The display begins in late winter, often even in late February, with the first blossoming of crocus and violets and extends through the asters and mums of late autumn. A number of flowering plants grow throughout spring and summer, including azalea, morning glories, trumpet vines, and butterfly weeds. Water lilies and floating hearts add color to the many ponds, while pink

Marsh grass and reeds provide food and homes for Delaware wildlife.

and white hibiscus dot the marshy areas. Some swampland is almost impassable because of the thickets of wild blueberry and cranberry.

Delaware also has an abundance of wildlife, mostly the animals that are common to the eastern United States, including deer, rabbit, mink, otter, both red and gray foxes, muskrats, and raccoons. Diamondback terrapin live in marshy areas near the coast, and snapping turtles are common in and around swamps. Amphibians such as frogs, toads, and salamanders also live in the damp areas around water or on wet forest floors.

Amphibians like this marbled salamander make their homes and lay their eggs in Delaware's damp areas.

A killdeer sits on its nest. If a predator comes too close, the killdeer will pretend to be injured and lead the animal away from the nest.

Wherever you are in Delaware you are never far from water—the ocean, Delaware Bay and River, the many rivers and streams, and about fifty small lakes and ponds. This brings a great variety of birds to the state, including shore birds, and makes birdwatching a favorite pastime.

At Bombay Hook National Wildlife Refuge near Smyrna, 275 bird species have been identified within the 16,000-acre refuge. This amazing number includes songbirds common to the East—bluebirds, robins, cardinals, and many others. Bombay Hook is also a stopping point for migrating shorebirds, including nine species of egrets, as well as ibis, heron, and a variety of ducks. Similarly, the dunes of Fenwick Island State Park are popular for observing black skimmers, osprey, and piping plovers.

Both the salt water and many sources of fresh water provide a great variety of fish. You can watch people surf fishing on the Atlantic beaches. You can also see chartered boats heading out to deep-sea fishing for flounder, rockfish, or weakfish. Closer to shore, the coastal waters provide shad, sea trout, and striped bass, and you often see people clamming or crabbing. Fresh water fishing at the state parks is also popular, with good stocks of bluegill, perch, largemouth bass, and catfish.

A fisherman releases a rainbow trout that he caught in one of Delaware's rivers.

Caring for the Environment

By the 1970s, the tremendous growth of Delaware's cities and suburbs, and the increase in factories and motor vehicles were filling the air with a yellowish haze. In the waterways, the harvest of fish and shellfish dropped off so sharply that many commercial fishers were forced out of the trade.

The Delaware state government passed several laws in the early 1970s in the hope of reversing these trends. It became one of the first states to establish a department of natural resources and environmental control. In 1971, the Coastal Zone Act stopped the building of any industrial plants along the state's coast.

In spite of these efforts, the quality of air and water continued to decline. This was partly because the state's population doubled between 1950 and 1980. A government study in 1989 showed that 63 percent of Delaware's lakes, rivers, and streams were not safe for fishing or swimming, and 80 percent of the state's people lived in areas where the air did not meet federal standards. Delawareans were even more stunned to learn that only two states in the entire nation ranked below Delaware in the study.

Since 1989, the people and their state officials have worked hard to make Delaware one of the nation's leaders in cleaning up air, water, and land. Strict laws have been passed to correct and regulate a variety of problems. These include garbage incinerators, landfills, underground gasoline storage tanks, and toxic waste from factories. Automobiles have to meet rigid emission standards and service stations have to sell a special non-polluting gasoline during the summer months.

Many families enjoy boating in the Delaware River.

Delaware

In addition, Delaware is working with five neighboring states to explore new ways to reduce air pollution.

These efforts produced encouraging results by 2000. Some dangerous pollutants, like lead, have been almost completely removed, while others, including soot, dust, and carbon monoxide have been sharply reduced. Water quality is also returning to pre-1970 levels. The beaches are again safe for swimming, and fishing is making a comeback.

Delawareans are also determined to preserve both wetlands and beach sand. According to James Matthews Jr. of the Department of Environmental Control, "We worked first on stopping erosion of the beaches and dunes. Since about 1998, we've spent more time and money on replenishing sand. Beach conditions are better now than they were a century ago." Fragile sand-dune ecosystems are now off-limits to pedestrians as well as motor vehicles.

Wetlands and swamps can no longer be drained until approved in a series of government hearings. Wetlands are also being protected by the state's efforts to increase the size of state parks. State-park acreage has more than doubled since 1990, and more than 1,000 acres have been set aside as wildlife preserves. Delawareans have done much to protect the beautiful land they call home.

Plants & Animals

Diamondback Terrapin

These medium-sized turtles receive their name from the raised plates on their shells. The female is larger than the male, with shells that measure about 9 inches. Terrapins are common in the marshes near Delaware's long beachfront.

Least Tern

Least terns are members of the gull family, but they are smaller and more graceful than seagulls. The terns' small size led to their name—the least of the terns. In flight, the forked tail and long, pointed wings give a tern a sleek, streamlined look.

Beach Plums

In early autumn, you might spot a few beach visitors harvesting the beach plums that grow in abundance on low bushes in the sand dunes. The bright blossoms of spring have turned into a small, tart fruit, that can be made into a thick, tasty jam.

Bald Cypress

Forests of bald cypress are common in the swamps of the Southeast but Delaware's Cypress Swamp is the farthest north that you will find them. The cypress is easy to identify by the bald "knees" that protrude above the water. Bald cypress are cone-bearing but they lose their needles like other deciduous trees.

Muskrat

When you see muskrats plowing across ponds, they look very much like small beavers. A muskrat has brown fur, slightly webbed feet, and a broad, flat tail. In fact the Natick Native Americans called them musquash, or musk beaver.

Eastern Tiger Swallowtail

These black and yellow butterflies can be found in Delaware's fields and trees from May through August. They feed on the nectar from flowers. Before they become butterflies, tiger swallowtails move around as green caterpillars with bright spots.

2 From the Beginning

History seems to be everywhere in Delaware. In one small town after another, you find carefully preserved village greens, old mills with stone grinding wheels, and even some old roads paved with cobblestones. In the larger town of Laurel, you can see 800 Victorian houses, displaying the elaborate architectural details known as "gingerbread." Delawareans are enormously proud of these reminders of the past and they work hard to preserve and protect that heritage.

Under Four Flags

For many years before the first Europeans arrived, the land was home to small bands of Native Americans. The largest group were known as the Lenni Lenape, but gradually they came to be called the Delaware. The Lenni Lenape lived in small semi-permanent villages, each containing a few families. They lived by farming as well as hunting, fishing, and harvesting shellfish.

When the first Europeans (twenty-eight Dutch settlers) arrived in 1631, the Lenni Lenape were friendly to them and

This group of children worked as berry pickers on a farm near Seaford around 1910.

showed them how to grow corn, beans, and squash. After a quarrel over stolen property, however, the Native Americans destroyed the settlement, killing all the colonists. That turned out to be the only warfare between Native Americans and European colonists in Delaware.

Residents of the present-day town of Lewes often call their town "the first town in the first state," because it was here that a group of Dutch settlers had hoped to start a colony in 1631. That early settlement was named Zwaanendael, which meant Valley of the Swans.

In 1931, residents of the town constructed the Zwaanendael Building. This structure, with elaborate stonework and steep gables, is a copy of a town hall in the Netherlands.

But in 1638, a group of Swedish settlers established the first permanent colony—New Sweden— near present-day Wilmington. They also built Fort Christina, named for their queen. Their leader and first governor was Peter Minuit, a Dutchman who had been dismissed as the governor of New Netherland (later known as New York). The Swedes made a permanent contribution to American life, especially the Westward Movement, by constructing the first log cabins. These were simple structures made of rough logs. This style would be used by American pioneers for the next 250 years.

An illustration of Swedish settlers landing in Delaware around the 1600s.

In 1651, Dutch from New Netherland established a claim to the land by building Fort Casimir at the future site of New Castle. The Swedes drove them out, but the Dutch stormed back and took control of the colony. Dutch control did not last long, either. In 1664, a powerful English fleet, sailed into Delaware Bay and quickly persuaded the Dutch to surrender.

In 1681, to satisfy a debt, the Duke of York—an English noble—gave a huge tract of land to William Penn, who established the colony of Pennsylvania. A few years later, the three "Lower Counties" of Pennsylvania asked to be separated and to form their own government. Penn agreed, and the three lower counties became the colony of Delaware in 1704.

A visual reminder of this unique history can be seen in New Castle. The old Court House there displays the flags of all four nations that controlled the area at different times—Sweden, the Netherlands, Great Britain, and the United States. Although Delaware separated from Pennsylvania in 1704, it was not until 1775 that the boundaries were firmly established.

William Penn addresses Swedish colonists in New Castle.

Revolution

Delaware played an important part in the American Revolution and the establishment of the United States as an independent nation. No major Revolutionary War battles were fought in Delaware, however, except for one brief fight in the north shortly before the battle of Brandywine in Pennsylvania. The British then occupied Wilmington for a time, and the Delaware state government moved to Dover for safety.

One of Delaware's great contributions was the formation of the "Delaware Line"—a regiment that served in the Continental Army under General George Washington. They became known as the "Blue Hen Regiment" because of the breed of gamecocks they took with them. (Cockfighting was a popular sport and people bet on the outcome, something like betting on horse races. It has since been outlawed in most states.) The 4,000 men who served in the Blue Hen Regiment proved their courage and fighting ability in battle after battle. One of Washington's officers commented that "They're the only soldiers I've seen who can fight all day and dance all night." One of their officers, Captain Robert Kirkwood, was reported to have risked his life 33 times before he was killed in battle.

Delawareans were also of vital importance in the decision to declare independence. First, John Dickinson used his persuasive writing and speaking to convince many Patriots that the time had come to declare independence from England. He became known as the "Pen of the American Revolution."

John Dickinson was a well-respected patriot who helped the revolutionary cause.

A problem developed at the Continental Congress in Philadelphia when the time came to vote on the Declaration of Independence in early July of 1776. The vote of the Delaware delegation to Congress was needed for the Declaration to be approved. But the delegation was split, and one member, Caesar Rodney, was home in Dover. When word of the problem reached Rodney, he knew what he had to do. Riding through the night at top speed, he made the 86-mile journey in time to break the tie in the Delaware delegation and win approval for the Declaration of Independence on July 4th. Rodney later became Delaware's second governor. In 1998 he was honored by having his ride etched on the new Delaware quarter.

The colonies won their independence in 1783. After experimenting with a national government that possessed too little power, a Constitutional Convention was held in Philadelphia in the summer of 1787. The new Constitution still had to be ratified, or accepted, by the voters of the thirteen states. Many people worried that the new national government would be too strong. Delawareans had no such concerns and, being such a small state, it was easy to hold a convention quickly. This enabled Delaware to become the First State—the first to ratify the Constitution. This is how the state got its nickname.

The 1800s

Throughout the colonial period and the early years under the new Constitution, Delaware was primarily a farming state. The fast-moving streams and rivers provided water power for mills, and this helped make Delaware an important center for processing foods which were sold in nearby cities, especially

Many Delawareans worked at the mills built along the state's waterways. These mills were on Brandywine Creek.

Philadelphia and Baltimore. In 1802, the duPont family started a gunpowder mill on the banks of Brandywine Creek near Wilmington. Throughout the 1800s and early 1900s, the duPont mills produced most of the nation's gun powder.

During the War of 1812, Delaware was in danger of British attacks, especially in 1814, when the British sailed into both Chesapeake Bay and Delaware Bay. Although the British landed and burned Washington, D. C., Delaware was spared. When British Captain Beresford fired on the town of Lewes, the townspeople picked up the cannon balls and shot them back. You can still visit the "Cannonball House," which displays one cannonball that remains lodged in a wall. The only casualties of this battle were a dead chicken and a wounded pig.

In the 1800s, communities like New Castle became busy trade centers. New Castle was an important marketing and shipping center, but it suffered a setback when the business district was destroyed by fire in 1824. Today, much of New Castle's early architecture that was not destroyed in the fire remains, including several historic houses open to the public.

In the 1860s, tensions between the north and south led to the Civil War. One of the main reasons for the war was slavery. Slavery had existed since the time of Dutch control, but it became less and less important in the early 1800s. There were no large plantations in Delaware and it was the plantations of the South that created the need for slave labor. Most Delaware slave owners voluntarily freed their slaves well before the Civil War. The slave population declined from 8,900 in 1790 to 1,800 in 1860.

As a state midway between the North and South, however, many Delawareans had strong ties to the Confederate cause. (The Confederacy was made up of the eleven southern states that seceded—or withdrew—from the United States. Members of the Confederacy were called Confederates. The northern states were part of the Union.)

The governor's mansion in Dover, called Woburn, was once a station, or safe house, on the Underground Railroad. This was the secret road to freedom for slaves in the years before the Civil War

For example, although Delawareans wanted to preserve the Union, they did not vote for Abraham Lincoln. Lincoln was running for president, and eventually led the North. And after the war, Delawareans felt bad for the southern states that were restricted by harsh government policies against the South.

In the years after the Civil War, trade and manufacturing became more important. Delaware mills produced not only flour and gunpowder but a variety of products, including cloth and paper. The city of Wilmington became a center for both manufacturing and trade. The rivers and the Chesapeake and Delaware Canal were used to transport manufactured goods and agricultural products. From the late 1830s on, railroads steadily grew in importance and water transportation declined.

Farmers bring wagons of watermelons to load onto the railroad cars near Laurel.

These young children worked in a cannery in Sussex County around 1910. Until strict laws were made and enforced, millworkers worked in dangerous conditions.

The Twentieth Century

In the twentieth century, industry changed in many ways—and the lives of Delawareans changed with it. The use of new sources of power, including steam and electricity, led to new industries in the Wilmington area. Factories made ships, railroad cars, machinery, and gunpowder. These industries were important for America during World War I, which lasted from 1914 to 1918, and World War II, which lasted from 1939 to 1945.

Women also helped war efforts by serving in the military. These women worked as pilots at the New Castle Army Air Base near Wilmington.

DuPont's gunpowder was particularly important and the company supplied much of the gunpowder used by Americans and their allies. The increased production in these factories provided jobs for many Delawareans. While many men fought overseas, women in the United States served their country by working in factories, shipyards, and other industries that helped the war effort. Many Delawarean women worked at jobs not available to them before the war.

Delaware has continued to change since World War II. DuPont and two related companies turned from gunpowder production to chemicals, such as paints and other household products. Most of the heavy industries have been replaced by light industry, such as food products, medical instruments, and electronic components. Delawareans work hard to make sure that their state continues to adapt to the changing times.

Important Dates

1609   Henry Hudson, sailing for Netherland, explores Delaware Bay and claims the entire area for the Dutch.

1631   The First European settlement in Delaware is settled by twenty-eight Dutch colonists.

1638   Swedish colonists establish the first permanent European settlement at Wilmington.

1664   The British take control of New Sweden.

1682   The Duke of York grants what is now Pennsylvania, including New Jersey and Delaware, to William Penn.

Henry Hudson

1704   William Penn allows three lower counties to have a separate government. The Delaware colony is formed.

1775   The "Blue Hen Regiment" joins the Continental Army.

1776   Cesar Rodney rides from Dover to Philadelphia and casts the deciding vote for the Declaration of Independence.

1778   John Dickinson drafts the Articles of Confederation.

1787   Delaware becomes the first state to ratify the Constitution.

1802   The duPont family establishes a gunpowder mill.

1838   Railroads connect Philadelphia and Baltimore encouraging industrial development in northern Delaware.

E.I. du Pont

1914–1918   World War I stimulates Delaware's industries.

1941–1945   World War II expands Delaware's industries.

1978   Large-scale busing is started to achieve integrated schools.

1981   Changes in state laws draw thirty large banks to establish offices in Delaware.

1984   S.B. Woo is elected lieutenant governor of the state. At the time, he was the United States' highest-ranking Asian American official.

2000   Delawareans elect their first woman governor—Ruth Ann Minner

3 The People

Only four states have fewer people than Delaware but, because of its small size, it has a high population density, or number of people per square mile. The population density, in fact, is among the highest in the country—401 people per square mile, compared to the national average of 69 per square mile. The state is far from crowded, however, since the total population is under one million. This means that Delaware has fewer people than many cities in other parts of the country.

Delaware has seen a remarkable mixing of peoples since the first Europeans arrived in the early 1600s. Even before 1700, the original residents—the Native Americans—had witnessed the arrival of settlers from the Netherlands, Sweden, and Finland, followed by England in the 1660s. In addition, small numbers of slaves were brought from Africa and sold to colonists.

According to the 2000 Census, about 75 percent of Delawareans are white. Nearly 20 percent are African American.

A young Delawarean enjoys the surf along Sussex County.

37

Families from many different cultures have made Delaware their home.

Asians account for less than 1 percent; and Native Americans represent about one-tenth of 1 percent. People of Hispanic descent make up nearly 5 percent of the state's population.

The Mixing of People

The makeup of Delaware's population changed a great deal during the 1700s. One change was the sharp decline in the Native American population. The villages of the Lenni Lenape, (later known as the Delaware), were almost eliminated, mostly by European diseases, like smallpox. Much of the Native Americans' land was taken over by European and American settlement. Most of the Native Americans in Delaware moved west, joining other Native American groups beyond the Appalachian Mountains. By 1750, only a few thousand Native Americans remained. The Nanticokes, the only remaining group of the Delaware, live in central Delaware and number about 500 people.

Powwows and other festivals are held throughout the year in different parts of the state. This Native American dances at a powwow in Riverdale.

The People

Lenape Straw Game

This straw game is a fun blend of skill and chance.

What You Need

15 paper straws or long lollipop sticks (found in craft stores)
Black or red paint
A small paintbrush
A crochet hook or a sharp pencil

Paint the straws with these patterns:

Paint one straw with stripes.
Paint one straw with a solid color on one end and stripes
    on the other end.
Paint two straws with dots.
Paint two straws with dots at each end, leaving the center blank.
Paint two straws with stripes at each end, leaving the center blank.
Paint two straws with a solid color at one end and leave other end blank.
Paint two straws striped on one end, with dots on the other end.
Leave three straws blank.

Once your straws are dry, begin playing the game. To play, the first player gathers the straws and tosses them down on a blanket or rug.

With the help of the crochet hook or pencil, the player tries to lift a single straw using his or her fingers without moving any other straws. (The Lenape used a bent quill to help them lift the straws.) A player earns points when a straw is successfully lifted.

Points system:

Straw with stripes: 75 points

Straw half solid and half striped: 50 points

Each of the straws two with polka dots: 25 points

Each of the two straws with dots at each end: 20 points

Each of the two straws with stripes at each end: 15 points

Each of the two straws solid at one end, other end blank: 10 points

Each of the two straws striped at one end, dots at other end: 5 points

The three blank straws: 1 point

When the player moves a straw other than the targeted straw, then his or her turn ends, and he or she adds up the points earned.

The next player gathers all straws and proceeds in the same manner. Play ends and a winner is declared when a player reaches 100 points.

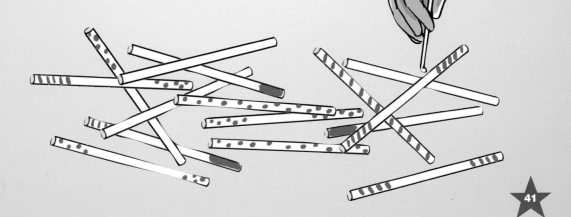

As the Native American population declined, the white population increased. The 1700s brought newcomers called the Scots-Irish people from Scotland who had tried settling in Ireland, then migrated to America. In the early 1800s, troubles in Europe brought two new groups. First came large numbers from Ireland, where a blight had destroyed the potato crop—the only source of food for most poor families. They came to America hoping to start over. German immigrants arrived in the 1840s and 1850s, driven from their homeland by political upheaval. Many native-born Americans disliked the newcomers because their language and customs were so different. This prejudice made it difficult for both Irish and Germans to find jobs and places to live. By about 1900, however, both groups had melted into the mainstream of American life.

In the late 1800s, the development of industry, especially in and around Wilmington, drew a new wave of immigrants from Southern and Eastern Europe. Poles, Slavs, Jews, Italians, and other groups came, many to work in factories, others on the railroads.

A Mixing of Religions

The very first European settlers represented different Protestant religions. The Dutch belonged to the Dutch Reform Church, while the Swedes were mostly Lutheran. The English brought a third Protestant group—the Episcopal Church. Small groups of Quakers also came to Delaware from Pennsylvania. The Quakers were members of the Society of Friends. Although few in number, the Quakers had a strong influence, especially in helping the people of Delaware see that slavery was wrong.

Events across the state celebrate the heritage of Delaware's residents. Delawareans dress in traditional Italian clothing for a festival in Wilmington.

The People

In the late 1700s, many Episcopalians fell under the spell of Methodist preachers and organized a new church—the Methodist Episcopal Church, which soon became the largest in Delaware.

Delaware After 1900

America's involvement in World War I and World War II led to a sharp increase in city populations, especially in Wilmington. Large numbers, including many African Americans from the South, came to work in the factories and shipyards.

After World War II, many people left Wilmington for its suburbs. Many newcomers to the state also moved to the suburbs. Today about half of Delaware's people live within commuting distance of Wilmington.

Between 1950 and 1960, Delaware experienced its largest population growth. The continued development of the state's chemical industry drew scientists, technicians, and other workers from other parts of the United States and from other countries.

Location also has something to do with why people move to Delaware. Most of southern Delaware remains rural and reveals the same kind of mixing of peoples that the state has experienced throughout its history. In Kent County, for example, you will find prosperous dairy and potato farms operated by Polish-American families who moved there from Long Island. At Iron Hill, there is a large group of people from Finland who came after World War I. And near Dover, there is a small Amish settlement, recognizable by their continued preference for horse-and-buggy travel and farming without modern, motor-powered machinery.

Delaware

An Amish farmer works in his field using his horses and a traditional plow.

The People

Famous Delawareans

Thomas Macdonough: Naval Officer

Born in what is now Macdonough, Delaware, in 1783, Thomas Macdonough gained fame in the wars against the Barbary Pirates from 1805 to 1807. During the War of 1812, Macdonough was placed in command of a small fleet on Lake Champlain, with orders to hold off a British invasion fleet coming south from Canada. Macdonough captured the British fleet, and saved New York and Vermont from invasion.

Annie Jump Cannon: Astronomer

Annie Jump Cannon was born in Dover in 1863 and became an astronomer at the Harvard Observatory. She gained fame for developing a system for classifying stars. She published her results in a huge nine-volume catalog. Her system is still used throughout the world and helped to make astronomy a more important branch of science.

The duPont Family: Chemists and Business Leaders

State history and the duPont family have been closely connected for 200 years. The duPont gunpowder mill on Brandywine River was built in 1802 by a French named Eleuthére Irénée du Pont de Nemours. The family business prospered into the 1900s, becoming the major supplier of America's gunpowder. The company also made nylon, paint, and other chemical products. Later members of the family served as state leaders in business, education, government, and the development of cultural institutions like the Winterthur Museum.

John P. Marquand: Author

John P. Marquand was born in Wilmington in 1893. After serving in the army in World War I, he became a successful writer of popular fiction. Some of his novels, and several stories, appeared in the Saturday Evening Post, *including a series about a Japanese detective named Mr. Moto. His novel,* The Late George Apley, *won a Pulitzer Prize, then became both a popular Broadway play and a movie. His later novels were also successful.*

George Thorogood: Musician

George Thorogood was born in Wilmington in 1950. Thorogood and his band The Destroyers made one of their first live performances at the University of Delaware in 1973. Over the years, the band recorded many albums and performed with other famous musicians and bands such as the Rolling Stones and BB King. Thorogoood and the Destroyers continue to tour around the country sharing their music with their fans.

Howard Pyle: Artist

In 1853, Howard Pyle was born in Wilmington. Pyle studied art and in 1876 had his first illustration published with a poem. Pyle continued to create beautiful illustrations for magazines and books and also worked on murals and other paintings. Praised for his artwork's historic accuracy and detail, many artists came to Delaware to study with Pyle. Pyle died in 1911.

Working Together for Education

For many years, education in Delaware was not unified throughout the state. While the early colonists valued education, nearly all schools were operated by the churches, so the quality of the education was uneven. Around 1700 wealthy English families began sending their sons to schools in England. They educated their daughters at home or at boarding schools in Philadelphia.

The state established a fund for schools in 1792, and a number of towns established public schools. Attempts to create a unified system were not successful until 1920, when a public school system was established. At the same time, a member of the duPont family donated a large sum of his own money to improve the schools.

During the 1950s and 1960s, African Americans protested against racial segregation in the schools. This was a problem that troubled schools throughout the nation. Following instructions from the U. S. Supreme Court, Delaware began creating greater racial balance in its schools in the 1960s. School desegregation was achieved although there was still tension over busing African-American students to all-white schools.

Education is an important issue for many Delawareans.

A father and his sons enjoy the cool waters under a waterfall near Brandywine Creek.

All Delawareans have worked together to achieve racial balance in the schools and to reduce racial tensions. By 1981, city and suburban districts were combined and busing has worked more smoothly.

Delaware has three state-supported universities and several private colleges. Since the state is too small to support professional schools, like medicine and architecture, arrangements have been made for Delaware students to receive advanced training at universities in Pennsylvania and other states.

As the state's population grows and changes, Delawareans will continue to work together to deal with issues that affect the state's residents.

Calendar of Events

The Delaware Kite Festival

With ocean breezes to help, hundreds of kites of every size and shape soar above Henlopen State Park on Good Friday for the Delaware Kite Festival.

Fashion Promenade

Held on Easter Sunday at Rehoboth Beach, the Fashion Promenade recalls the 1890s with fantastic displays of bonnets and other clothing worn for the Easter Parade in Victorian days.

Old Dover Day

Held on the first Saturday in May, Old Dover Day celebrates the city's rich heritage, with stately old homes (including the birthplace of Annie Jump Cannon), the State House, Legislative Hall, and just south of town, the John Dickinson Plantation.

Wilmington Garden Day

During Wilmington Garden Day, held in June each year, visitors can tour some of the most famous and elegant gardens in America, including the gardens at the Winterthur Museum and the Nemours Mansion.

A Puerto Rican festival and parade

50

The Victorian Ice Cream Festival

In July, the Victorian Ice Cream Festival is held in Rockwood, featuring fancy concoctions and the atmosphere of ice cream parlors of the late 1800s.

Delaware State Fair

July is the month for the Delware State Fair at Harrington. The fair offers traditional displays, like farm produce and cattle, as well as a gigantic fireworks show.

Nanticoke Indian Powwow

This colorful event, held each September near Oak Orchard, includes Native American costumes, crafts and foods.

Brandywine Arts Festival

In September, the Brandywine Arts Festival draws artists and art to an area noted for the paintings and illustrations of Delaware artist Howard Pyle.

Fall Harvest Festival

The Fall Harvest Festival takes place in late October at the Delaware Agricultural Museum in Dover. The event features advances in farming science and technology, as well as the products of Delaware agriculture.

A Nanticoke at a powwow in Millsboro

How It Works

Rules to Live By

The constitution of a state is its framework of government. It describes how the government of the state will be set up to meet its three functions: the legislative function—making laws; the executive function—running the affairs of the state; and the judicial function—a system of courts that settle disputes or hear cases when laws are broken.

During America's colonial period, the legislature in each colony could make its own laws, but the English king could reject any law he did not approve of. In 1776, when the Continental Congress approved the Declaration of Independence, the thirteen colonies became thirteen independent states and could write their own state constitutions. The voters of Delaware had a constitution ready by the end of 1776.

Over the next hundred years and more, three new constitutions were written. The constitution in use today was written in 1897. But Delawareans have made changes, or amendments, in the constitution more than 100 times. Amending the constitution

The state legislature meets at the state capitol.

is easier in Delaware than in almost any other state. The change must be passed by two sessions of the legislature, with an election in between those sessions. The governor cannot veto the amendments and Delaware is the only state in which the changes do not have to be submitted to the voters.

From Bill to Law

As in other states, before a law is passed in Delaware, it must go through an established process. Most laws begin with a suggestion or an idea from a Delaware resident or a member of the state legislature. The proposed law is called a bill.

The four flags of the nations that each ruled Delaware fly from the balcony of the Old Court House in New Castle.

Once a bill is introduced to one of the two houses, it is assigned to a committee. The committee members examine the bill, hold meetings or hearings, or revise the bill. The committee can reject the bill and decide not to present it to the entire house. But if the committee is satisfied with the bill, it is presented to the entire house.

Branches of Government

Executive The governor is the head of the state. He or she is responsible for approving or rejecting laws passed by the legislative branch. The governor prepares the state budget, and suggests new laws. Along with the lieutenant governor, the attorney general, and the treasurer, the governor is elected to a four-year term.

Legislative The legislative branch, called the General Assembly, is divided into two houses. Twenty-one senators are elected for four-year terms, and forty-one members of the house of representatives serve two-year terms. The General Assembly passes bills which, when signed by the governor become laws. If a measure is vetoed, a three-fifths vote of both houses can override the veto.

Judicial All judges are appointed by the governor with the approval of the senate. These judges serve twelve-year terms. The highest court, the Supreme Court, hears appeals from lower courts and can decide that a law is unconstitutional if it violates some part of the state constitution. Below the Supreme Court is the Superior Court, for criminal cases, and the Court of Chancery which hears cases involving civil rights and corporations. The lowest courts are called magistrate courts, presided over by justices of the peace, who usually have no training in law. These are local courts that hear cases involving matters like family disputes or minor law breaking.

The bill is read to the house three times. After the second reading, legislators can revise or amend the bill. They usually debate the bill after the third reading. After the third reading and the debates, the legislators vote on the bill. If it is approved, it is sent to the other house. There, it goes through a very similar process.

If both houses agree on the bill, it is then sent to the governor. If the governor approves the bill, he or she can sign it into law. The governor can make changes to the bill and send it back to the General Assembly. If the governor does not take any action, the bill will automatically become law after a certain amount of time. The governor can also veto—reject—the bill. The vetoed bill can still become law if two-thirds of the members of both houses vote to override the governer's veto.

Local Government

The counties—New Castle, Kent, and Sussex—are the primary units for local government. New Castle and Sussex governments consist of an elected council and council president. Kent county uses an older system. They have an elected board of commissioners called the "levy court." The name comes from the old tradition of levying or collecting taxes.

In addition, large towns and cities generally elect a mayor and a council. A few hire a city manager rather than a mayor. Two towns in the north—Arden and Ardentown—have town meetings and operate according to the ideas of Henry George, George was an author of the 1890s. In this system, the townspeople retain the title to all land. In other words, they own the land together, rather than individually.

Delaware

Citizen Leadership

Because Delaware has so few people, which means limited income from taxes, it has sometimes been impossible to take on expensive projects. In the 1820s, for instance, Delawareans knew that a canal to connect the Delaware River and Chesapeake Bay would be good for business. The canal would make it cheaper and faster to transport products. They had seen how the recently completed Erie Canal across New York State had reduced the cost of shipping farm products by 90 percent. But Delaware's General Assembly had just established a fund for schools and there was no money left for a canal.

Business and plantation owners decided to do it on their own. They raised money, formed a company, and built the Chesapeake and Delaware Canal. The 15-mile canal was completed in 1829. It quickly became the most important canal in the state. With locks to raise and lower ships, the canal made it possible to ship farm products from central Pennsylvania to Chesapeake Bay. From the Bay, the products could travel by sea to any port on the Atlantic Coast. In 1919, the federal government bought the canal and deepened it for ocean steamships.

A similar story took place in the early 1900s. The development of the automobile created the need for paved roads, especially running north-south. The farms and towns of southern Delaware were becoming increasingly isolated from the faster-paced life of the northern corner of the state. Since there was no money in the state budget, T. Coleman du Pont, a member of the state's famous business family, undertook the task with his own money in 1911. The four-lane road was completed in 1924, and duPont then turned it over to the highway department as a family gift to the state.

Products are transported through the Chesapeake and Delaware Canal.

 58

Delaware

These are just some examples of how residents can work together to improve their state. Most Delawareans are not able to use their own money to build roads or canals, but they can still take an active part in their state. They can stay informed on the state issues and what the government is doing about them. If they have a problem or an idea for a new law, they can suggest it to state legislators. Together with their legislators, residents can work together to make a difference.

If you would like to get in touch with Delaware's state legislators, go to this Web site: http://www.legis.state.de.us/Legislature.nsf/? and click on General Information.

5 Making a Living

Farms, Mills, and Waterways

The morning mists rose above the streams and rivers of northern Delaware, as the sun glistened on the lapping water of mill wheels, while the steady power of the water turned large stone grinding wheels. This quiet scene was repeated every day through the early 1800s. Farm wagons would drive up to the stone mill houses with loads of corn to be ground into meal or wheat into flour. Mills were also used for cutting lumber, and for making paper and textiles. One of the early mills, established on the Brandywine Creek in 1802, was used to manufacture gunpowder.

The early settlers built their farms and plantations close to the rivers and streams to make use of the waterways for transportation. There were few roads in Delaware until the 1900s, so transportation by horse-drawn vehicles was slow, and boats or sailing ships were more convenient.

A young Delawarean picks strawberries on his family's farm near Viola.

In the colonial years, many of Delaware's farms and plantations had grown tobacco as a cash crop—a crop to sell for income. Sailing ships could pick up the product from the docks and transport it to markets in Europe. Tobacco rapidly wore out the soil, however, and Delawareans searched for new sources of farm income. Many in the northern part of the state turned to wheat, while corn became the major crop in southern Delaware. The mills were developed to serve these new crops.

Around 1830, peaches were introduced in Delaware, and this marvelous fruit, imported from China, created a great wave of prosperity for the state's farmers. The crops were shipped by the waterways. After 1840 they were sent by railroad to city markets, especially Philadelphia and New York. But the peach boom did not last. The peaches were stricken by a blight—a disease—called the "yellows" and the orchards declined steadily after 1900.

Combines harvest the barley on a farm near Federica.

Recipe for Peach Kuchen

Ingredients:

For the crust:

1 stick unsalted butter

1/4 cup sugar

1-1/2 cup flour

1/2 teaspoon salt

1 teaspoon vanilla

1 teaspoon baking powder

1 egg

To make the filling:

5 peaches

1/2 cup sugar

1 tablespoon cinnamon

Ask an adult to help you preheat the oven to 350 degrees Fahrenheit. While the oven is heating up, mix together the butter and sugar for the crust. Add the rest of the crust ingredients and mix. The dough should be crumbly, but it should still hold together. Spread butter or margarine on the sides and bottom of a 9-inch pan. Press the dough into the pan and up against the sides.

Peel, remove the pits, and cut the peaches into slices. Lay the peach slices on the dough. Sprinkle the peaches with cinnamon and sugar. Bake at 350 degrees for 25 to 35 minutes, until the crust is a golden brown.

Have an adult help you remove the kuchen from the oven—it will be hot. When it is cooled, add a little ice cream or whipped cream and enjoy.

Since about 1870, agriculture has undergone several changes. The development of industry, beginning in the late 1800s, became a larger source of income, but farming has remained very important. As the peach orchards declined, many farmers turned to growing fruits and vegetables for city markets. Crops like beans, peas, tomatoes, berries, and melons were shipped by water or rail; today these farms, many operated by part-time farmers, are called "truck farms," since road transportation has replaced railroad and ships.

By the late 1900s, the tremendous growth of urban areas has given farmers ever-expanding markets. The large markets along with the development of refrigerated trucks and the construction of super highways, has led many farmers to discover high profits in raising chickens. Actually they raise broilers. These are chickens five to twelve weeks old. These chickens are used for cooking. By the year 2000, broilers were the largest source of farm income in Delaware, with roughly 200 million sold each year. This addition has helped to make Sussex County one of the wealthiest counties in the nation.

Today the southern two-thirds of Delaware continues to display some of the most picturesque and valuable farmland anywhere. Sussex County in the south of Delaware is one of the wealthiest agricultural counties in the country. In addition to corn and wheat, soybeans have become a major crop, and, in the south, potatoes. Farm families in the extreme south also make holly wreaths during the Christmas season. Mixed with the cropland and truck farms are the dairy farms, featuring a colorful variety of herds—Holstein, Guernsey, Jersey, and Ayrshire.

Young Delawareans prepare their cows for a livestock show in New Castle.

Making a Living

Products & Resources

Chemical Research

In 1938, the announcement of the creation of nylon by DuPont scientists caused a sensation worldwide. Nylon is a durable substance that can be spun as fine as silk. It even replaced silk during World War II in the manufacture of parachutes. This break-through in the development of synthetic materials led dozens of chemical companies to establish research laboratories in Delaware.

Broilers

Raising chickens has become the largest source of agricultural income in the state, and Delaware farms have about 250 million chickens. The young chickens make up 95 percent of the annual agricultural sales.

Ocean Beaches

Rehoboth Beach and Bethany Beach are the most popular ocean resorts in the state. They are an easy drive from Pennsylvania, Maryland, and New Jersey, and visitors from all over relax on the sandy beaches on sunny days. The coast of the Delaware Bay is home to other smaller beaches that locals enjoy.

Truck Farms

Delaware's bridges and roads have given farm families easy access to city markets. Truck farms, located in Kent and Sussex Counties grow table vegetables, like lettuce, tomatoes, broccoli, beans, peas, and squash. Fruits, including berries and melons, are particularly popular.

Museums

The Winterthur Museum near Wilmington is one of the most famous in America, with about 200 rooms displaying furnishings, architecture, ceramics, and metalwork, all dating before 1840. The Hagley Museum on Brandywine Creek, located in the old DuPont gunpowder mill, offers a history of American industry. In addition, entire sections of some towns, like the Old Court House area of New Castle, are outstanding "living museums" of buildings from the 1700s and 1800s.

Hogs

Many farms across the state raise hogs. Hog farms sell their livestock to companies across the state and throughout the country. Some of the livestock is sent to meat processing plants in Delaware. The hogs are used for ham, bacon, and other pork products.

Commercial fishing remains profitable, although the pollution problems reduced the number of fishing boats. Fishing boats and chartered boats are used to catch saltwater fish in Delaware Bay and the ocean. Shellfish harvesting along the coast is profitable as well.

The DuPont Story

In 1802, the arrival of a French immigrant and his father marked a turning point in Delaware's history. The immigrant, named Eleuthere Irenee du Pont de Nemours, persuaded his father to finance the building of a mill to manufacture gunpowder. The high quality of the product made the company a great success and it rapidly became the country's largest supplier of gunpowder and one of the largest in the world. From the early 1800s on, Eleuthère Irénée du Pont de Nemours and Company has been a mainstay of Delaware's economy. In addition, family members in each generation have been major participants in the state's cultural and political life.

In 1912, the federal government said that the duPont Company was a monopoly in the manufacture of gunpowder. That means that the company controlled so much of the industry that there was no longer any competition. As a result, DuPont was divided into three corporations: Atlas, Hercules, and DuPont.

Over the next few years, duPont abandoned most of the gunpowder production and turned to the development of chemical products, like paint and dyes. All three companies made the Wilmington area a major center for chemical research and for administration of the sprawling manufacturing operations. In the mid-1930s, DuPont chemists made a product out of water and air combined with a by-product of coal to create a substance they called nylon. Nylon, of course, proved to be a great economic success widely used as a fabric to make clothing, parachutes, and other products. The success of nylon also showed the advantage of research in petrochemicals—products that make use of petroleum or coal.

The DuPont laboratories and a manufacturing plant helped to make Wilmington an important industrial center. The city's location is also ideal for business. Waterways, railroads, and highways placed northern Delaware within easy reach of Philadelphia, Washington D.C., and other cities. The major highways and railroads pass through the Wilmington area from Pennsylvania and New Jersey on the north and east and into Maryland on the south and west. In fact, Wilmington is within 150 miles of four of America's ten largest cities.

Manufacturing

Although Wilmington could claim to be the "chemical capital of the world," other manufacturing concerns have moved into Delaware since 1900. Food processing is now second only to chemicals in economic importance. Large plants in Dover, for example, make gelatin, puddings, and other dessert products. Other plants in

A researcher uses a magnifying glass to inspect parts in a Delaware research facility.

northern Delaware make baked goods, fish products, and soft drinks; poultry processing has become more important every year. The completion of the Delaware Memorial Bridge in 1951 provided an important link with Maryland and New Jersey, leading major automobile companies to set up assembly plants in Delaware.

Manufacturing plants along the Delaware River can have ocean ships load and unload at the factory's dock, without needing railroads or trucks.

Government and Tourism

Government is also a major source of employment, including state and local government offices, schools, and two major military facilities—Dover Air Force Base and Fort Miles Military Reservation.

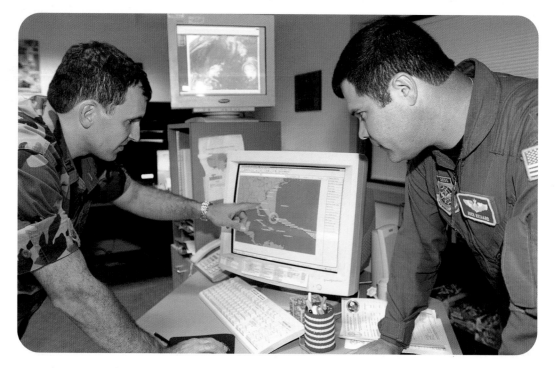

Military personnel at Dover Air Force Base monitor a hurricane that is approaching the Delaware coast.

Many visitors to the state come to enjoy the beaches and the clear waters of the bay, rivers, lakes, and streams. The parks and forests are excellent for hiking, mountain biking, or camping. Others come to the state to see the historic sites that honor Delaware's—and the nation's—history.

Festivals, fairs, and other events often draw a number of people to Delaware. The state has a number of museums and galleries where people can admire artifacts, art, and other unique treasures. Tourism in Delaware brings in tax dollars as well as providing jobs for state residents. The steady growth of tourism creates a wide variety of jobs in service industries, including restaurants, hotels, and motels.

A family enjoys a day at the beach.

"The Home of Corporations"

In the mid-1900s, Delaware's business and government leaders wondered what they could do to attract new business to Delaware. There was only so much room in the state for industries and Delaware has no natural resources for industry like coal or iron ore. In fact, the state ranks last in the country in mineral production. In addition, the state's small population did not offer a large pool of workers.

The state leaders came up with an unusual solution. They changed the tax laws and corporation laws to make it easy and

Industries helped to build and develop Delaware.

profitable for companies to establish corporate offices in Delaware—even though their major operations were in other parts of the nation or the world. Dozens of corporations took advantage of the laws and set up offices in the Wilmington area and Delaware had a new nickname—"the Home of Corporations." In the 1980s, similar changes in the state's laws led banks and credit card companies to come to the state. Today, an estimated 200,000 banks and corporations have at least a legal connection to Delaware. These developments have enabled the state government to reduce personal income tax rates four times since 1995. At the same time, the need for offices and housing has contributed to steady growth in the construction industry.

Delaware's economy continues to grow and change with the times. As more people move to the state, the cities and suburbs will continue to expand. The workforce and the state industries will also keep growing, helping Delaware move into the twenty-first century and beyond.

DECEMBER 7, 1787

The state flag is blue with Delaware's coat of arms (the image from the state seal) inside a buff-colored (yellowish) diamond. The date of Delaware's statehood is printed beneath the diamond.

Delaware's state seal includes the state's coat of arms in the center. The coat of arms is made up of images of a farmer (to represent farming), a militiaman (to represent liberty), an ox (to represent the importance of livestock), water (to represent the Delaware River), corn and wheat (to represent agriculture), and a ship (to represent shipbuilding and the coastal economy). Below these items is a banner with the state motto. Along the bottom of the seal are three years: 1704 is the year that Delaware's General Assembly was established, 1776 is the year of American independence from Great Britain, and 1787 is Delaware's year of statehood.

State Flag and Seal

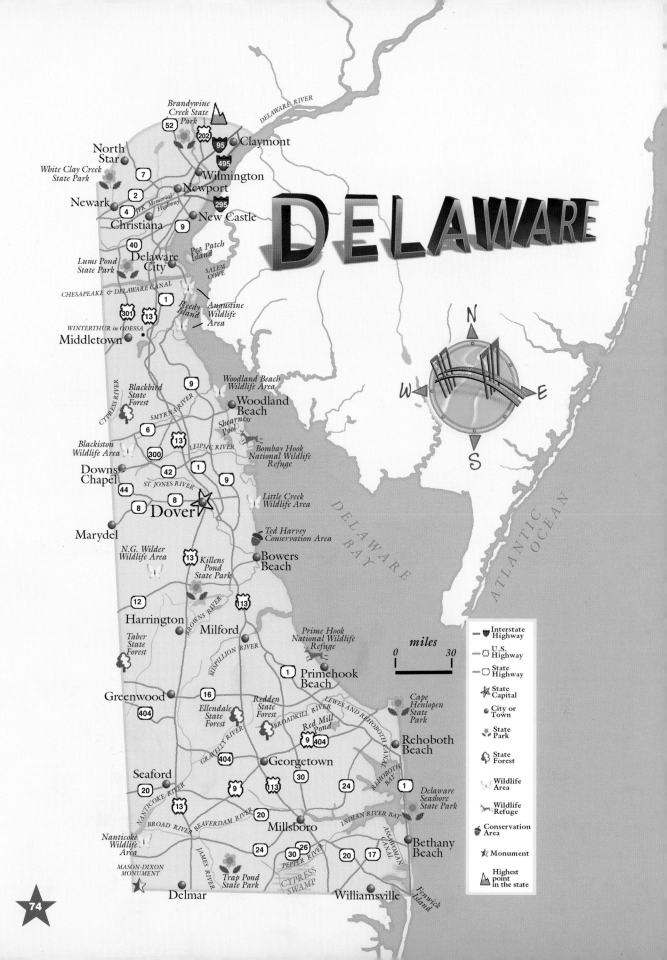

DELAWARE

Brandywine
Creek State
Park

52

202

95

Claymont

DELAWARE RIVER

North
Star

495

White Clay Creek
State Park

7

Wilmington

Newport

2

295

Newark

4

JFK Memorial Highway

New Castle

Christiana

9

40

Delaware
City

Pea Patch
Island

Lums Pond
State Park

SALEM
COVE

CHESAPEAKE & DELAWARE CANAL

i

Reedy
Island

Augustine
Wildlife
Area

WINTERTHUR in ODESSA

301

13

1

Middletown

9

Blackbird
State
Forest

Woodland Beach
Wildlife Area

CYPRESS RIVER

SMYRNA RIVER

Woodland
Beach

Shearness
Pool

6

13

LEIPSIC RIVER

Blackiston
Wildlife Area

300

Bombay Hook
National Wildlife
Refuge

Downs
Chapel

42

1

44

ST. JONES RIVER

9

8

Little Creek
Wildlife Area

8

Dover

Marydel

N.G. Wilder
Wildlife Area

Ted Harvey
Conservation Area

13

Killens
Pond
State Park

Bowers
Beach

12

BROWN'S RIVER

113

Harrington

Milford

Prime Hook
National Wildlife
Refuge

Taber
State
Forest

MISPILLION RIVER

1

Primehook
Beach

Greenwood

16

Cape
Henlopen
State Park

404

Ellendale
State
Forest

Redden
State
Forest

BROADKILL RIVER

LEWES AND REHOBOTH CANAL

Red Mill
Pond

GRAVELLY RIVER

404

Rehoboth
Beach

404

Georgetown

30

Seaford

9

113

24

REHOBOTH BAY

1

Delaware
Seashore
State Park

20

NANTICOKE RIVER

13

20

Millsboro

INDIAN RIVER BAY

ASSAWOMAN CANAL

Nanticoke
Wildlife
Area

BROAD RIVER

BEAVERDAM RIVER

24

30

26

20

17

Bethany
Beach

MASON-DIXON
MONUMENT

JAMES RIVER

PEPPER RIVER

CYPRESS
SWAMP

Trap Pond
State Park

Delmar

Williamsville

FENWICK ISLAND

DELAWARE BAY

ATLANTIC OCEAN

N
W   E
S

miles
0   30

Legend
- Interstate Highway
- U.S. Highway
- State Highway
- State Capital
- City or Town
- State Park
- State Forest
- Wildlife Area
- Wildlife Refuge
- Conservation Area
- Monument
- Highest point in the state

Our Delaware

Words by George Hynson
Music by William Brown

More About Delaware

About the State

Blashfield, Jean F. *The Delaware Colony*. Chanhassen, MN: Child's World, 2003.

Brown, Dottie. *Delaware*. Minneapolis, MN: Lerner, 1994.

Miller, Amy. *Delaware*. Danbury, CT: Children's Press, 2002.

Thompson, Kathleen. *Delaware*. Austin, TX: Raintree Steck-Vaughn, 1996.

Web Sites

Kids Corner—The Delaware Tourism Office:
http://www.visitdelaware.com/kidscorner.html

The Official Website for the First State:
http://www.delaware.gov

Delaware Kids Page:
http://www.state.de.us/gic/kidspage/kidspage.htm

About the Author

David C. King is an award-winning author who has written more than forty books for children and young adults. He and his wife, Sharon, live in the Berkshires at the junction of New York, Massachusetts, and Connecticut. Their travels have taken them through most of the United States.

Index

Page numbers in **boldface** are illustrations.